Young
Reggie Jackson
Hall of Fame Champion

A Troll First-Start® Biography

by Andrew Woods
illustrated by Allan Eitzen

Troll Associates

Library of Congress Cataloging-in-Publication Data

Woods, Andrew.
    Young Reggie Jackson: Hall of Fame champion / by Andrew Woods;
illustrated by Allan Eitzen.
       p.   cm.— (A Troll first-start biography)
      Summary: A biography of the Yankee batter who broke Babe Ruth's
record by hitting three home runs in a row in the 1977 World Series.
    ISBN 0-8167-3762-2 (lib. bdg.)   ISBN 0-8167-3763-0 (pbk.)
     1. Jackson, Reggie—Juvenile literature.   2. Baseball players—
United States—Biography—Juvenile literature.   [1. Jackson,
Reggie.   2. Baseball players.   3. Afro-Americans—Biography.]
I. Eitzen, Allan, ill. II. Title. III. Series.
GV865.J32W66   1996
796.357'092—dc20   95-10020
[B]

Reggie Jackson is one of the most famous
baseball players in history. He once hit
three home runs in one World Series
game! Only the great Babe Ruth had ever
done that before.

Reginald Martinez Jackson was born on
May 18, 1946.

Reggie grew up near Philadelphia, in a town
called Wyncote.

Reggie, his parents, and his 5 brothers
and sisters lived above the family's busy
dry cleaning and tailor shop. All the
children helped out.

When Reggie was 6 years old, his parents separated. His mother moved away with some of the children. Reggie and two brothers stayed with his father.

Reggie was happiest when he was playing
sports. He was good at every sport he
tried. He liked practicing with his dad.

When he was 13 years old, Reggie's baseball team played in a school championship series against a team from Florida.

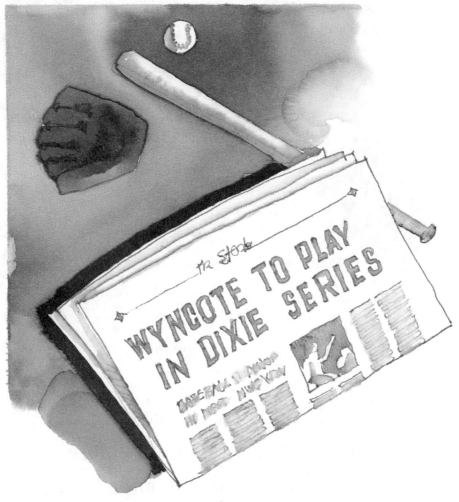

WYNCOTE TO PLAY IN DIXIE SERIES

Reggie was the only black player on his
team. This had never mattered before.
But now the coach said he couldn't play.

10

Reggie was upset. He never thought that
he was different from anyone else. He was
the team's best player and really wanted to
play in the big Series.

11

Finally, in the last game of the Series, the coach let Reggie get up to bat. Reggie was so nervous he couldn't think.

Strike One! Strike Two! Strike Three!
Reggie had struck out.

Reggie felt as if he had let everyone down.
After that day, Reggie was determined to
show everyone he could make it to
baseball's major leagues.

Reggie got good grades in school. He was also a star on his high school's basketball, baseball, football, and track teams.

Reggie's best sport was football. He received a scholarship from Arizona State University to play football *and* baseball. After his first year at college, Reggie decided that baseball was more important to him than football.

In 1966, at the end of his sophomore year,
all the major-league teams wanted Reggie
to play baseball for them.

Reggie signed a contract with the Kansas City A's for $75,000. The A's also offered him $2,000 a semester so he could finish college.

Reggie played in the minor leagues for 2 years. He moved up to the major leagues in 1968. By then the A's had moved to Oakland, California.

Reggie played for the Oakland A's for 8
years. In the beginning, he struck out a lot
and the fans booed him.

Reggie practiced hard. In his third season he hit 47 home runs. He was becoming known as a power hitter.

In 1972, the Oakland A's made it to the
World Series. But Reggie couldn't play.
He had injured his leg during the play-offs.

The next season, Reggie returned and played so well that he was voted Most Valuable Player.

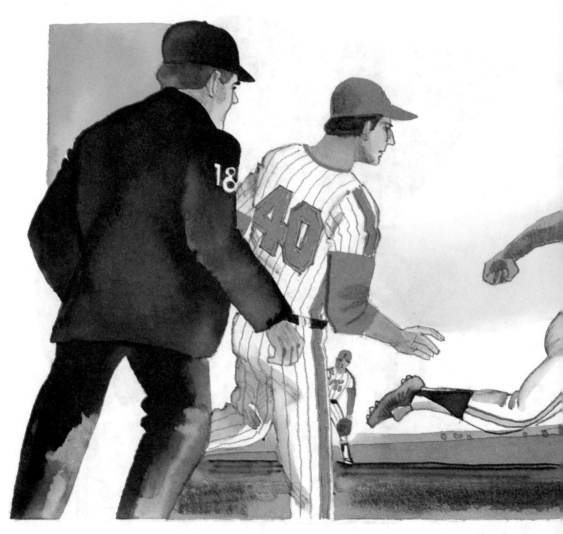

The A's were in the World Series again.
Reggie hit a two-run homer in the final
game to help the A's win the Series.

In 1974, Reggie helped his team win the
World Series for the third time in a row.

Reggie joined the Baltimore Orioles in 1976. He liked his new team, but he really wanted to play for baseball's most famous team: the New York Yankees.

In 1977, the Yankees offered Reggie
almost 3 million dollars to join them. Some
of the other Yankees thought Reggie was
being paid too much. But Reggie would
soon prove he was worth the money.

That year, the Yankees made it to the
World Series. In the final game, Reggie hit
3 home runs in a row as the Yankees won
the game and the World Series.

The Yankees began the next season by
losing many games. Then the team
magically pulled together and started
winning! They won the World Series
again.

Reggie seemed to hit home runs
whenever the team needed it most. His
teammates called him "Mr. October"
because that's when the World Series was
played—and when Reggie was at his best.

After 5 years with the Yankees, Reggie decided
to return to the Oakland A's. He played with
them until he retired from baseball in 1988.
In 1993, Reggie Jackson was inducted into
the Baseball Hall of Fame. "Mr. October"
had earned his place in baseball history!